LeRoy Neiman

# BIG-TIME GOLF

# BIG-TIME GOLF

HARRY N. ABRAMS, INC., PUBLISHERS,
NEW YORK

Editor: Sharon AvRutick
Designer: Tom Bentkowski

*Library of Congress Cataloging-in-Publication Data*

Neiman, LeRoy, 1927–
    Big time golf / LeRoy Neiman.
        p.    cm.
    ISBN 0–8109–3666–6
    1. Neiman, LeRoy, 1927–   .   2. Golf in art.   I. Title.
N6537.N39A4   1992
759.13—dc 20                                           92–8037
                                                         CIP

Printed and bound in Japan

# CONTENTS

uring the '30s, hard upon the Great Depression, golf meant little or nothing to a kid growing up in St. Paul.

Apart from sneaking on the public courses at Como Park and Phelan Park to hit a few balls around before being shagged by the pro or green-keepers, for my friends and me it was body-contact team sports that

prevailed. Our matchups were limited more or less to sandlot baseball and football and church basement boxing.

More equality was shown through the more socially graceful pastimes of the long sub-zero Minnesota winters, where everyone, regardless of economic level, shared and romped in the crystal pristine ice and snow. Speed skating, figure skating, cross-country skiing, and ski jumping were de rigueur, and the Winter Carnival fun and games helped tide us over the frigid months.

The Twin Cities, St. Paul and Minneapolis, provided few athletic events that merited national attention. Spectator sports consisted primarily of minor-league baseball and minor-league hockey and the then-awesome University of Minnesota football.

Every stifling-hot summer, however, the city did host a rather glamorous big-time golf tournament that lured the major players of the day to swat golf balls and mosquitoes at the Annual Greater St. Paul Open held at Keller Golf Course. Keller presented a gentle rolling terrain with lush green, tree-lined fairways and was said to be "well trapped."

"Light Horse" Harry Cooper and Horton Smith used to duel there just as they did at The Masters in 1936. Cooper won the first St. Paul Open in 1930, and Smith, the second in 1931; Cooper took

7

it again in '35 and '36, and Smith repeated five years later.

I was off to war in 1941 and never really got back to St. Paul and lost track of the St. Paul Open, which was junked in the late '60s. Checking the history of the tournament, I discovered that four of the great stars I've included in this book were winners there: "Slamming" Sam Snead in 1937 and again in 1949, Jimmy Demaret in '48, Doug Sanders in '62, and Ray Floyd in '65. Keller also hosted several PGA tournaments.

Golf was something special, I'm sure, in the Twin Cities back then, because Bobby Jones won the US Open in 1930 at Interlachen in Minneapolis, and Minneapolis-born Patty Berg dominated women's golf.

Galleries wore fashionable knickers, argyles, and caps like the players, as well as straws and panamas; the ladies favored the cloche. Some players wore long-sleeve shirts and ties. Who influenced whom, I used to wonder. Was golfers' attire reflecting casual wear of the day or was *it* the influence?

Anyway, that was a big-time scene for me and my introduction to big-time golf.

What discouraged my developing my own game? Here's one good explanation. After serving two years in the ETO, one in combat during World War II, I voluntarily served a year's duty in the

Army of Occupation as an Army artist. During this impressionable time an incident kept recurring that affected me in such a way as to put my golf game permanently on hold. You see, GIs were allowed the privilege of playing the resort course at Bad Nauheim, Germany—that is, unless General Patton was playing. No matter what hole you were at—be it 6 or 15—when the General teed off for his round, every enlisted man was kicked off the course by our own MPs.

True, that's small excuse for my not working on my game, a game at which I, of course, considered myself a natural, but it did help channel my energies to concentrating on my art.

Being an Army artist was a good deal. At the time I was specializing in doing VD posters, and my career stretched out promisingly before me with the GI Bill educational benefits awaiting my return. My work gained top priority at the expense of sports activities.

But in the early '70s I got back to golf not by hitting balls, trying to lower my handicap, but rather when I hit on the splendors of world-class golf and its premier players and courses. I got into depicting rather than playing, with a steady gaze fixed on big-time golf.

## THE DRAMA

Golf, not unlike painting, consistently requires patience, decisiveness, calculation, concentration, and self-reliance.

It is an individual sport, an intermittent, pedestrian sport. It can be therapeutic, psychological, and—oh yes—frustrating, always advancing the ball, no backing up.

Golf is a civilized activity. The tour golfer is a gentleman. He signs in, clean-shaven, at the first tee of a tournament on Thursday and is never seen showing up for the final 18 on Sunday with a day's growth of beard or wearing a fierce scowl meant to be threatening or intimidating. He's playing the course, not against someone else.

He tallies up his own score and hands his card in at the scoring tent at the close of each round—responsible and respectful of the rules. He calls infractions on himself. Integrity is an unwritten rule of the game.

Golf is not a perspiring art, unless play is under a scorching, blistering sun; unless the leader, after holing out on the final round, is sweating out the arrival on 18 of the closest runner-up; or unless a rookie, in a state of anxiety, is teeing up on his premier round at Augusta.

Golf is a quiet game in most respects, meant to be pacific. Gallery mavens are reminded to be silent by marshals holding "Quiet" signs high, and sportscasters whisper into their mikes when near the action. The sounds of nature hold

sway—the birds, the wind, the rustling of leaves, maybe the sound of surf, or sometimes raindrops pattering on open umbrellas.

Profanity is held to a minimum. The pro mouths his discontent under his breath, reprimanding himself for an unsatisfactory shot. But the ever-present TV cameras read lips as they zoom in on his every move and expression while tracking the flight and roll of every ball.

Only on Mondays' lucrative corporate outings is the big-time golfer spared the critical eye of reproving galleries and the ever-present network television crews.

Undaunted, the pro performs public feats with as few strokes as possible under competitive pressure, whatever the conditions. His only aim is to measure up to his own demanding standards.

All in all, it all really hinges on a beautiful, compact, consistent swing. Wasn't it Duke Ellington who coined "It don't mean a thing if you ain't got that swing"?

# THE PLAYERS

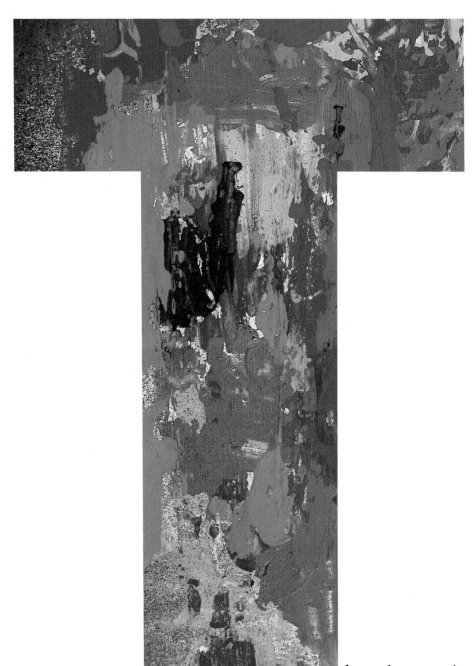

he players, it goes without saying, are the focus of big-time golf outings. There are certain expressions in general that pass over the faces of the tour pros off the tee. First off, while smartly steadying themselves, feet carefully spread, they glare down at the little white sphere they are preparing to clout—to murder it, if you will. Ball beware!

At the top of their swing their facial muscles are held taut. Then the killer grimace tightens as the club descends violently with every ounce of power that can be mustered. Swiftly, viciously, the head of the weapon slams into the ball. The player's fierce expression remains fixed as the ball soars up and out into space… gaze steady, following the flight—lips drawn tightly back, teeth bared, much the same as with a downhill skier in motion.

A long, straight drive will bring out "Oooh" from the gallery. The player, now having bent over and retrieved his tee, smiles to himself then tersely nods in agreement to and acknowledgment of their polite applause.

If a poorly driven shot falls short of expectation or veers off the fairway, a teed-off expression of anguish will register his disbelief.

As he proceeds along the fairway, the player's range of ritual expressions becomes more calculating and cunning with each stroke up to the green. At the eventual theater-in-the-round, a loyal audience awaits the entrance on stage of the cast. The players proceed as to a script, busy themselves with milling about, gleaning, circling, measuring, policing, and plucking the green carpet, setting the stage for the dramatic roll to the hole. This brings about the final expression, that of satisfaction or frustration, exuberance or disgust—it all depends.

Jerry Pate—US Amateur and US Open titlist in 1974.

Overleaf: "The Shark," Greg Norman.

Legends of golf
(upper left to right):
Sam Snead,
Ben Hogan,
Gary Player,
Lee Trevino,
Arnold Palmer,
Jack Nicklaus.

Overleaf:
Golf winners
(clockwise from
upper left):
Hal Sutton,
Arnold Palmer,
Seve Balesteros,
Tom Kite,
Jack Nicklaus,
Tom Watson.

The painting was
created for *The
Wonderful World
of Golf* by Mark H.
McCormack
(Atheneum,
New York, 1973).

LeRoy Neiman '84

Curtis Strange—
back-to-back US
Open winner ('88
and '89).

Johnny Miller—
"The Desert Fox,"
blasting out
of sand.

Tammie
Green

Marie - Louise de Lorenzi
victoire dans l'Open Britanique féminin

# TWO TWOSOMES

Our own Tammie Green and Marie-Laure deLorenzi of France, two talented topnotchers.

The South Dakota brothers Curt (the older) and Tom Byrum have a lot in common.

U.S. Open 1990
Wykagyl Country Club
New Rochelle NY

Betsy King

LeRoy Neiman '91

## WOMEN DRIVERS

**Opposite: Betsy King performs wonders. I saw her, well ahead, sink an eagle putt on the final hole at New Rochelle, N.Y., in the 1990 Big Apple Classic.**

**Left: Nancy Lopez captivated the public's heart, the most popular and important player among the ladies. Shot a 20 under par at the Henredon Classic in 1985 (66-67-69-66).**

**Above: Jane Blalock answered to "Tomboy Blalock" growing up in New Hampshire. A top LPGA player in the '70s.**

## PIONEERS

Pete Brown was the first black to win a PGA tournament, the San Diego Open in 1964. Many others followed—names like Jim and Lee and Calvin—distinguished winners and front-runners all. A crop of young phenoms is now on the rise.

**Above: Calvin Peete**—he has some big wins. Frequently a front-runner or in contention.

**Right: Lee Elder**—first black to play in the Masters. Once shot a 61 final round in a tournament.

**Far right: Jim Thorpe**—6 feet, 200 pounds, Mississippi-born. Some players hit a bullet, but with Thorpe it's a shot out of a cannon.

Lee Elder

Jim Thorpe

Steady star
Calvin Peete on
the fringe.

Opposite: Jim
"Distance" Dent—
longest hitter on
tour in the '70s. Has
more club than
most other Seniors.
This 1975 painting,
*Black Power*,
includes an
all-white gallery.

Calvin Peete
'83

LeRoy Neiman

Seve

LeRoy Neiman

'90

# SPANISH NOBILITY

Opposite:
Internationally
admired Spaniard
Seve Balesteros,
winner of two
green jackets and
three British
Opens, among his
over 50 victories.

José Maria
Olazabal, popular
winner who plays
golf chivalrously
with flamenco
finesse.

Right: Ireland's Christy O'Connor, Jr., Ryder Cup star and World Cup player, driving at the Galway Bay Golf and Country Club at Oranmore, Galway Bay, on the coast of western Ireland. For me, west Ireland means Jack B. Yeats (1871–1957), the great expressionist painter who was brought up at Sligo Town in west Ireland, locale of the marvelous County Sligo Golf Club.

Opposite: Preeminent golfer of 1990, Nick Faldo "The Brit"— English star who once spent a semester at the U. of Houston. Back-to-back Masters wins in '89 and '90.

Below: Ian Woosnam, 5' 4½", Welshman "Woosie," winner of the '91 and '92 Masters, is the cigarette-smoking ordinary man's player.

# TWO BRITS AND AN IRISHER

A sunny, shady, Sunday summer scene. Under a harsh, brilliant afternoon sun, Ian Woosnam is in the process of making a fine shot. The sunlight flickers through the trees, reflecting colors from above and all around on the figure, blending it into the surroundings. The whole thing brings to mind Matisse's Mediterranean paintings. The figure emerges out of the scattered colors.

Doug Sanders

Lee Trevino

LeRoy Neiman '91

## SENIORS

Pure Texanese threesome: It all started way back in the '30s when Jimmy Demaret brought in a new era of golf—the flavor of Texas—by flaunting an explosive personality, spectacular clothes, and outrageous statements.

Low-key knickers, broadcloth shirt, necktie, and argyle socks were out. The stylish Demaret introduced clothes no one had ever seen on a golf course and won The Masters 3 times.

Not to be outdone, colorful Houstonian Doug Sanders, 20 times a PGA winner, 2 times a British Open runner-up, added a playboy life-style. His color-coordinated wardrobe makes him the reigning peacock of the Senior fairways.

Next, the ebullient Tex-Mex from Dallas, Lee Trevino—winner in Canada, Mexico, Japan, Australia, the PGA, 2 US Opens—provided a flair for big occasions. No clotheshorse, the outgoing Super Mex is always entertaining to watch, always cheerful and articulate with that sensational flair for the dramatic. His huge galleries were soon named "Lee's fleas."

The players' seasoned personalities, affectations, and eccentricities are the very flavor and essence of the Senior tour.

The Senior tour was not organized for long-in-the-tooth players to be turned out to pasture—anything but. The quality of their play and their competitiveness says it all.

*Demaret - earthquake personality outrageous remarks*

Byron Nelson, another Texan, was born in 1912, the same year as his peers Ben Hogan and Sam Snead. Iron Byron won The Masters in 1937, the US Open in 1939, the PGA in 1940, and The Masters again in 1942.

His health prevented him from serving in the military during World War II, and he went on to win 54 tournaments on the tour. In 1944 he won 7 times and in 1945 11 times in succession.

Because of a bad back and a weak stomach Nelson retired at age 34 and only played in The Masters for pleasure thereafter, although he'd managed to win the French Open in 1955.

Even if Byron were around today the Seniors would have to do without his stellar game. He just wasn't your durable long-haul, gladiatorial golfer.

Chi Chi Rodriguez, "Zorro"—headed toward his 60s, 132-pound show-man—scored eight consecutive birdies on the 2nd round at the Silver Pages Senior Classic in '87.

Chi-Chi Rodriguez

LeRoy Neiman

Masters - Augusta '73

Arnold Palmer in Pink Shirt

LeRoy Neiman

**Arnold Palmer—silver gray and youthful, with over 60 wins in his 60 years.**

**At the bar in New York's 21 Club with Argentina's Roberto De Vicenzo, called "the Latin Snead." Winner of the 1967 British Open and more than 100 other international titles, among more than 230 total career victories.**

**Far right: Dave Hill —20 years on the PGA tour. Didn't drink or smoke until 1968. Has never been sick, insists his golf improved with imbibing and inhaling, and is leery of clean living and jogging.**

DORAL EASTERN OPEN

Blue Course
Doral Country Club
Miami, Florida
March 8 – 11, 1973

Dave Hill
Doral
3
11
73

LeRoy Neiman

Sam Snead teeing off at Vintage Palm Springs. On his left, Gary Player, and, right, Billy Casper, US Open and Masters winner, and Arnold Palmer. Billy recommended I trim his shape down to his proportions in his early years.

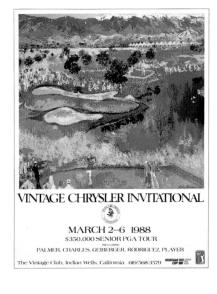

41

# GILDED YOUTH
# AND GOLDEN AGE

The beginnings and opportunities of these black Americans differ greatly.

Rising from near-impossible conditions, Charlie Sifford, who qualified for the tour in 1959, accomplished something that only a chosen few out of a thousand do—whatever their color. His example and achievements are for all to applaud, with the highly touted, encouraged, and carefully nourished California teenager Tiger Woods at the head of the line. It's different today, but so much the same—the same challenge.

**Cigar-chomping 70-year-old Charlie Sifford—getting on in years but having no trouble getting on the green.**

**Opposite: Teenager Eldrich "Tiger" Woods, 5′ 11″.**

Tiger Woods

## THE GRIP

It was said that Brooklyn Dodger Zack Wheat's viselike grip
(he was a lifetime .317 hitter) could reduce a baseball bat to
sawdust.

The golfer's firm grip of authority is his measure of control
over the club.

# KNICKERS

It seems in keeping with tradition that knickers have made a comeback and are worn by some of today's top players.

Payne Stewart's loose-fitting trousers gathered at the knees hark back to the Jones-Hagan-Sarazen epoch of the knickers.

Patty Sheehan's look makes a bold statement, bringing to mind the original English definition of knickers: "bloomer-like undergarment worn by women, or women's and girls' short-legged undergarment—panties."

**Payne Stewart—loud colors and confidence to match, which do not detract from his graceful swing.**

**Patty Sheehan—early 30s, dozens of career LPGA victories, including Japan LPGA championships back to back in the early '80s.**

Mike Tyson
Roadwork for Ruddock fight

5:15 A.M.

Dunes Hotel and Casino golf Course Neiman Las Vegas

2-16-'91

## BOXERS ON COURSE

Traditionally, prizefighters in training are often seen doing early-morning roadwork over the fairways of unpopulated golf courses. The peace, quiet, and open air are ideal.

1991: Mike Tyson jogging solo for 20 minutes over the Desert Golf Course of the Dunes Hotel and Casino in Las Vegas, readying for the 2nd Ruddock fight. He is tuned into his headset, running to the beat.

mickey
mantle

yankee stadium

LeRoy Neiman      Sept 29 '63

world series

Above: 1964 heavyweight champ Sonny Liston preparing for his first Cassius Clay fight, chugging over a Miami public course with his attendants.

The great retired heavyweight champ Joe Louis relaxing after a friendly Nassau round on the afternoon of the Clay-Liston rematch at Poland Springs, Maine, Golf Club in 1965.

Opposite: Baseball players take naturally to the feel of clutching a club and swinging away. Back in 1964, before a Yankees-Dodgers World Series game at Yankee Stadium, I caught Mickey Mantle pre-game, sharpening his putting stance with bat and baseball. Many of today's active high-income pro athletes take to golf and excel there as well. Big "perspiring arts" names like racecar driver Bobby Rahal and basketball superstar Michael Jordan have an interest in the game that extends far beyond mere big-time celebrity tournaments.

**Right:** With shotmaker Lanny Wadkins at Pebble Beach, where he won the PGA in 1977.

**Below:** At The Masters, chatting with former US and British Open champion Tony Jacklin.

**Above:** With good friend Raymond Floyd at Pebble Beach.

**Left:** Shaking hands with Nick Faldo at the 2nd of his back-to-back Masters wins in 1990.

Left: At Pebble Beach, Jack Nicklaus pointing to the 18th tee, telling me, "A good hole to pick up a birdie if you need one to win or to make a par to stay ahead."

Below: Nearby resident, actor Clint Eastwood on driving range at Pebble for the Crosby Celebrity, 1984.

Left: Picture player Arizona's Tom Weiskopf on the 1st tee at Oakmont. Winner of the British Open, one of the best ball strikers of all time.

53

# THE COURSES

Private club pro and his assistants demonstrating sand-trap techniques at a members' and guests' hypothetical club outing.

 long
and distinguished place in art history is held by landscape painting. In the
19th-century pastoral tradition, artists vigorously pursued the challenge of
painting the theme of the figure in a rural landscape. (They even got
around to painting the nude dwelling out-of-doors.)

Perhaps the most significant landscape painter who helped open the way to Impressionism was the earthy French master François Millet (1814–75), born of a peasant family. Millet dedicated his life to painting such subjects as farmers swinging scythes and toiling in the calm agricultural landscape.

The golfer swinging his club in today's golf landscape features the human presence in the serene countryside in much the same way.

The artist just doesn't walk out on a golf course with a sketch pad to portray a particular golfer, or tournament, or course. Straightaway, he is confronted by an awesome greenscape equally as intimidating and challenging to him as it is to the golfer on his mission.

The first impressions are those that stick. The eye is held by the vastness of the spatial effects—the overwhelming feeling of space, light, and air. The figure of the golfer is inseparable from and as one with the surroundings. Man and nature in concert.

The players advance the ball around the course, over natural ground and facing natural obstacles, while contending with the scheming transformations that the course architect contrived.

Along the fairway nature challenges, and then out of nowhere manmade hazards intervene and dominate. These innovations can be downright diabolical but serve to test the players' tenacity and shot-maker skills—everything from lakes to sand traps, graceful slopes to abrupt rock escarpments. Hazards include

Seve Balesteros in '88, putting at the Westchester Classic. Commissioned to do the tournament poster, I decided to depict Seve, and he then proceeded to win the tournament.

MANUFACTURERS HANOVER
WESTCHESTER CLASSIC
Westchester Country Club
August 13-19, 1979

gravelike bunkers, ditches, and water —all part of the essential character and grand design forming the golf motif.

Golf players humanize the field of play. Members suburbanize their landscape. In turn, the tour pros and tournament-goers urbanize the course.

The tour players look right in this environment. They fit, they belong, they're qualified—but the artist sees them differently from the spectators who follow them. The gallery's main concern is about birdies and eagles, the score, the lie, the players' form. What I am experiencing meanwhile is forms made up of patches of color and lines integrated in the landscape space.

There is no choice but to deal with the visual sensations.

Forget (ignore) the information about the players in the sports pages, their TV performances, and the leaderboard. All homework about yardage, greens contours, and the ever-present hazards is wiped out.

Let's take a beautiful day—the myriad of colors, the midday luminous brilliance of natural lighting that creates patches of unexpected broken color scattered over the ground and vistas. The Impressionist painters would have been in paradise. An arbitrary light source serves best for purely dramatic freedom and control.

First it's a landscape painting, then it's the figure in a landscape, and finally it's a golfscape.

## BIG-TIME PRIVATE GOLF CLUB

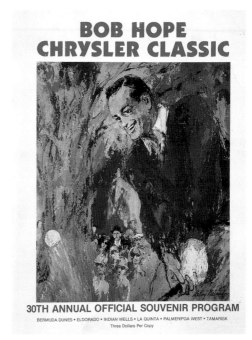

*The $2 Million World Country Club Golf Championship*

Edgewood Tahoe Golf Club
Stateline, Nevada
May 19-22, 1983

**CAESARS TAHOE**

Big-time golf country-club members are club-bable by nature—either being socially clubby or just clubbing the ball.

The heavy hitters in the clubhouse are seldom the heavy hitters off the tee.

For the better part, club chieftains are an association made up of the illustrious, the recognizables, the notables, the somebodies from the world of big business and mighty corporations.

Big-time private country clubs are primarily concerned with themselves. Club potentates believe they may be the last possessors of the secrets of exclusive living, being the perpetuators of a standard set by their wealthy predecessors. They are the preservers and keepers of the social advantages that go with being affluent and influential.

The monied classes (socially select) had the racket, links, and mallet action all to themselves until the working man and the professional man gained the leisure time and entered into the country-club scene, creating recreational environments of their own.

They took as their guidelines the rituals and organized play practices of the very rich as they developed their own country clubs.

In this era of increased leisure time the commercialization of pay-to-play golf for the

**BOB HOPE CHRYSLER CLASSIC**

30TH ANNUAL OFFICIAL SOUVENIR PROGRAM
BERMUDA DUNES • ELDORADO • INDIAN WELLS • LA QUINTA • PALMER/PGA WEST • TAMARISK
Three Dollars Per Copy

masses has arrived, along with a reluctant relaxation and breakdown of admittance restrictions and qualifications set by august country-club bastions. Increasingly, their memberships are becoming open to minorities.

It must be remembered, however, that the gracious elegance, style, and dignity that private clubs demand of their membership succeeded in establishing an atmosphere of refinement, a quality of behavior. Rules and etiquette are stressed and maintained in the manners and form of the gentleman. These sanctuaries of privilege have set an example for today's new breed.

The question is just who gains admittance to the costly goodies of the symbolic clubhouse, old or new. Another question is the symbolism of the clubhouse building in relationship to the golf course— subordinate to nature's character or in recognition of nature's dominance? In other words, is the building's role one of being incidental to the grounds, or are the grounds a setting for the building?

The country-club golf ball.

## GALLERIES AND SPECTATORS

Within the tableau of golf during tourney time, the average member of the public is allowed to walk the hallowed fairways of snobbish courses as a ticket-paying guest. Every weekend somewhere in the world mobile galleries of golf's devotees follow in the wake of the stars, and, for four days, the snubbable outnumber the snubbers.

The divot man.

Perched in the high rows of temporary bleachers, onlookers have a bird's-eye view of the birdies.

When a ball arrives on or near the green before the player comes in view, there is speculation and expectancy. Whose ball is it?

Hillside squatters, standees, and the stands stalwarts who have awaited each threesome's arrival clap in acknowledgment of the fine approach shot. Then the player is roundly applauded upon coming into view, reapplauded when recognized, striding briskly with his caddy, and cheered again as he arrives at his ball. Final applause is withheld until that distinct sound of the plunk of the ball in the cup is heard.

## ST. ANDREWS
## Birthplace of the Ball-and-Stick Game of Golf

It's said no red-blooded golfer's education is complete until he's played Old St. Andrews, with its crumbling fairways, hidden hazards, gigantic greens, sharp burrows and contours, raw weather, and shifting winds. The fabled old course, the heart and home of golf—"The Queen of Golf."

Wayfarers make pilgrimages to this monument to golf's origins, enshrined in royalty and tradition. The Queen of England is its patron, and Edward VII, Prince of Wales, was Captain of the club, affectionately called "The Old Lady" by locals.

St. Andrews is surrounded by the commanding beauty of the turbulent North Sea. Cliffs, golden beaches, and snow-capped highland mountains in the distance set off the time-worn buildings.

**Painting on the course.**

65

# MEMBERS OF THE R&A

## MEMBERS' CLUBHOUSE

From his vantage point inside the clubhouse of the hallowed Royal and Ancient, a governing member at the command post stronghold scans the terrain, keeping a surveillant eye on the course.

The true St. Andreian recognizes a friend at a distance by his swing, before he can make out his features.

## VINTAGE MEMBERS

Ardent old-timer and his faithful friend.

Strong winds make only a large dog suitable for making the rounds with his master. Strong winds are small-dog warnings.

They say you can buck the wind all the way to 9, then face it all the way back.

LeRoy Neiman '87

*Bullshit baffles Brains*

*Danny*
*caddy Old St. Andrews 78 years old*
*scotland*
*'87*

## CADDY

The Old Course caddy who shepherds the golf pilgrims is not a mere carrier of clubs. Traditionally, he is an expert in the game. His lineage is almost as old as the game and is cared about like a treasured heritage.

A foreign visitor once asked his caddy, "This is such an old course—does anyone know who designed it?" The caddy pointed to the sky. "T'was the man up there that did it."

The Old St. Andrews caddies are as rugged as the course itself. Their very roots are in the soil of this hallowed ground. Typical and loved, Jimmy Barrie is one of a kind of this special breed, sketched in billed tweed cap.

The use of the services of the St. Andrews caddy is part of the Old Course experience. To not take a caddy at Old St. Andrews is to deny oneself "the wine of the country."

They are advisory and speak their mind. A story goes that a caddy arrived drunk to accompany a tourist. "You're drunk," the man said. "I won't have a drunk caddy." The scathing answer: "Maybe I be drunk, but I'll get sober. You can't golf, and you'll never get better."

**LeRoy with caddy Jimmy Barrie.**

*Old St. Andrews*
*LeRoy Neiman '87*
*Jimmy Barrie caddy*

## GROUSE SHOOTING IN THE HIGHLANDS OF SCOTLAND

Scotland is a country of field sport. The grassy hill-pasture of the moorlands lures many a country sportsman to grouse shooting in the hilly highland heather-covered ground. Many Scotsmen prefer the exercise of "walking up the gorse over dogs" in the bracing air and high winds.

Often a single gun goes out by himself with his retriever in the same spirit as the golfer tramping over the wild shrub and thick growth of Old St. Andrews.

More secure than grouse and partridge —and much safer—are the numerous crows hopping along the course of Old St. Andrews, oblivious to the cross fire of golfers, not hunters, up and down the narrow fairways that run side by side.

The golf course in Scotland fits naturally into the texture of the land.

Elbow benders drink, toast, and pledge while having their pre- and post-round bracers and pick-me-ups in pubs and other premises licensed to sell liquor within a short iron of the Clubhouse.

It's said that you golf your way back into the city from the water at hole 9, like a salmon swimming upstream in Scottish waters.

## THE JIGGER INN BAR

"SPIKES ARE WELCOME"
      —sign on entrance

THE CADDIES' RETREAT
The Jigger Inn Bar, a place of renown,
It's known by the caddies as the best place in town,
It's clean and it's friendly, with plenty of cheer,
The service is great and so is the beer,
Let's drink to a pub, our place of retreat,
The best place in town, where most caddies meet,
A place to enjoy, it's all above par,
Thanks to the staff of the Jigger Inn Bar.

      *—excerpt from a poem on the taproom wall*

## ROYAL AND ANCIENT

"And still St. Andrews links with flags unfurled shall peerless reign and challenge all the world."

The Scots, so smitten with golf, caused St. Andrews to observe the Sabbath.

Old Tom Morris, 19th-century canonized golf great, said, "Nai Sunday play. The Old Course need a rest sir, if the golfers don't."

# LE GOLF EN FRANCE

Bonjour, la France! Bonjour, Paris! Bonjour, le golf de St.-Cloud!

La passion for golf has become a habit in France. The fever has hit. Golf not just as practiced in ultra-exclusive clubs, or by top-level tournament champions, but as a sport open to all, without any loss of the cherished snobbism of the French. The early courses in France were very much preserves for the aristocracy and the wealthy.

Just outside Paris is the enchanting St.-Cloud Golf Club. The charm and events of centuries past combine gracefully with the pastime of today's golf. Golf at magnificent St.-Cloud is a power walk through history.

St.-Cloud's history includes Catherine de Medici in the 16th century. Henry III took refuge at St.-Cloud in 1559 and against its backdrop was assassinated by a monk.

History continued to unfold at St.-Cloud when Henry IV was recognized as King of France, thus marking the beginning of the Bourbon dynasty.

In 1785, Queen Marie Antoinette bought the St.-Cloud château for her second son, Louis XVII, just born. When the revolution came, the royal family had to leave Versailles for the Tuileries in central Paris. St.-Cloud then became the official summer residence. In 1791, when the mob prevented them from leaving Paris for St.-Cloud, Louis XVI decided to flee with his family, with tragic results.

Napoleon Bonaparte was named consul for life in 1802, and the château became his favorite official residence. In 1810, the civic part of his marriage to Marie-Louise was celebrated, and their son Le Roi de Rome was born the following year.

Today a splendid part of that same glorious environment welcomes the armies of golfers to play.

**LeRoy on footpath from rear of clubhouse.**

**Overleaf: Bordeaux still life featuring special Le Bunker white.**

Golf de Saint Cloud

Graves          Médoc          Pauillac

LE BUNKER
GRAVES BLANC
APPELLATION GRAVES
1986
MIS EN BOUTEILLE
BORIE-MANOUX
A BORDEAUX FR

CHATEAU MARGAUX

ND VIN
DE
U LATOUR
GRAND CRU CLASSÉ
1969

of Bordeaux          LeRoy Neiman '91

## CLUBHOUSE BAR AT ST.-CLOUD

Conventionally in France, the members
do not hang out in the clubhouse as
members do in US clubs. This is chang-
ing, however, with social activities on the
rise. French clubhouses now resemble
the French casinos, which have so long
served as social centers.

3-23-68
LeRoy Neiman

Beer from the barrel
Endives
Jambon d'Ardennes

Royal Golf Club De Belgique Terrveren
Château de Ravenstein
Belgium

# BELGIUM

The Château de Ravenstein, the club-house of Le Royal Golf-Club de Belgique holds snobbish, justifiably so.

History has it that in the 16th century Philippe de Cleves, owner of a castle along the Flemish part of the river Meuse, then called Ravenstein, acquired some adjacent land on which he built a pavilion, which he and his pal the Duke of Burgundy used as a hunting lodge.

In 1905, King Leopold II, in his desire to promote golf in Belgium, officially founded Le Royal Golf-Club de Belgique. Today, the Château de Ravenstein houses the complete facilities of the clubhouse with its exclusive, highly selective membership. Chic and haughty, the château rules over a course that rates as one of the best in the world.

## GAVEA GOLF AND COUNTRY CLUB

The harbor city of Rio de Janeiro is famous for its unsurpassed grandeur, for the fashionable luxury hotels along the Copacabana to Leblon and Ipanema, and for the turquoise-green sea and the white sandy beaches decorated by glistening brown bodies.

Along with the exhilarating sensations and magic of Rio are its magnificent, kaleidoscopic range of mountains, and one of them, Gavea Mountain, is just a strong wood shot away from the heart of the city.

For their pleasure, the English fashioned the Gavea Golf and Country Club at the knees of Gavea Mountain. Here, the well-heeled play in the sensual languor of hot afternoons in their exclusive garden of delight.

**What appears to be a macaw, the emperor of parrotdom, is perched on his throne, robed in gorgeous plumage. These grand birds of gigantic size and beauty are amiable, gentle, and teachable. Naturally good tempered, they set a good example for the golfer.**

**Opposite: I painted an international foursome here simply because few great players have ever walked this course. So I put England's Nick Faldo, Spain's Seve Balesteros, Germany's Bernhard Langer, and Australia's Greg Norman on a course none of them has ever played.**

**Birdies and eagles at golf clubs here are represented by the macaw.**

**Sandal-clad Carioca caddies come from nearby destitute barrios of great poverty that are sandwiched between the lush, tropical greens and steep fairways of the posh Gavea grounds and the glass-and-steel palaces of modern Rio.**

LeRoy Neiman                                    Bahia Golf Course

LeRoy Neiman Hong Kong '90

## SHEK O COUNTRY CLUB
## HONG KONG

Midway between an opalescent dawn and a luminous Asian evening sky, a relaxing noontime pause on the patio as members lunch at the Shek O Country Clubhouse.

The Shek O Country Club, situated on a peninsula at the eastern end of Hong Kong island on Big Wave Harbour, flaunts a vista of the China Sea and distant mountain ranges.

Shek O has long been home to a small village of fishing
people plus a quite small, tony English expatriate community.
    The exclusive club founded by these strict traditionalists
has a Chinese and international membership according to
British rules.

# LADIES
## SHEK O COUNTRY CLUB

COURSE RATING 63·3

Player ..................................................  Competition ..................................................

Date ..................................................  Handicap ..................................................

| Marker | Hole | Yards | Par | H'cap. | Score | Points | + — O | Marker | Hole | Yards | Par | H'cap. | Score | Points | + — O |
|---|---|---|---|---|---|---|---|---|---|---|---|---|---|---|---|
| | 1 | | | | | | | | 10 | 273 | 4 | 2 | | | |
| | 2 | | | | | | | | 11 | 284 | 4 | 10 | | | |
| | 3 | | | | | | | | 12 | 151 | 3 | 16 | | | |
| | 4 | 162 | | | | | | | 13 | 243 | 4 | 12 | | | |
| | 5 | 244 | 4 | | | | | | 14 | 288 | 4 | 4 | | | |
| | 6 | 146 | 3 | 15 | | | | | 15 | 249 | 4 | 14 | | | |
| | 7 | 216 | 3 | 5 | | | | | 16 | 290 | 4 | 6 | | | |
| | 8 | 294 | 4 | 3 | | | | | 17 | 96 | 3 | 18 | | | |
| | 9 | 198 | 3 | 9 | | | | | 18 | 285 | 4 | 8 | | | |
| OUT | | 2013 | 31 | | | | | IN | | 59 | 34 | | | | |
| | | | | | | | | OUT | | 2013 | 31 | | | | |
| | | | | | | | | TOTAL | | 4112 | 65 | | | | |

Marker's Signature ..................................................

Player's Signature ..................................................

LESS H'CAP

NET SCORE

*Chinese guest YUF-Sai*

*LeRoy Neiman '90*

## AVOID SLOW PLAY
## PLEASE REPLACE ALL DIVOTS

**T. C. Chen,
Taiwan's man on
the tour.**

*Tze-Chung Chen
TAIWAN*

*T.C.*

*LeRoy Neiman '90*

86

Caddies for Barron Hilton's foursome SHEK O Country Club Hong Kong '90
LeRoy Neiman Big Wave Harbor

While Thursday is for women members and their guests, every day is women's day to the caddies. The elderly Chinese ladies wear the same type of straw hat that is worn by their peers weeding the paddies. They climb up the hill from the sleepy harbor below to tote bags. The young men of the village no longer want to do this type of work.

The Shek O caddy covers the ball in the fairway or rough with a red handkerchief so the crows don't dive for the ball.

## LANDSCAPE PAINTING IN CHINA

Chinese brush-painting technique admits no correction, no second chance. The artist stores observations in his memory, conceives and completes the mental image, and then transfers it swiftly with sure strokes to silk or rice paper in a personal and unique gesture.

In Chinese painting, rocks and stones, boulders and ledges have been interpreted as the bone and structure of the earth. The same holds true with the golf course.

A Chinese landscape painting can be filled with tempestuous forces, and a raging dragon can be depicted among the clouds possessed of power and grandeur seemingly at the point of bursting out of the picture—yet the elements of such paintings are controlled, integrated, and harmonious.

The Oriental painter selects a sable or monkey-hair brush as the golfer chooses his club, like no other could do the job. The club stroke is like a brushstroke—both are swift and sure.

## JAPAN—*GORUFU*

In this land of sake and sumo, golf prevails. *Gorufu*—latest Japanese addiction. Golf's global epidemic has spread to the new breed, *shinjinrui*, who value leisure and personal fulfillment above all. The *kaisha senshi*, corporate warriors, could well be the modern-day equivalent of the feudal samurai, with the golf course as the dueling ground.

Japanese stick-handling dexterity is marveled at worldwide. Witness the extraordinary martial art kendo. Legend has it the samurai warrior could catch a fly with chopsticks.

Today's competitive golfer smartly drawing his golf stick from his bag could well be a samurai warrior drawing his battle sword from its sheath.

It goes without saying those LPGA players are no slouches either at swiping, swooshing, and swatting with the golf shaft.

Ayako Okamoto

LeRoy Niemann '91

Edison N.J.

QUEEN'S CUP

日本女子プロゴルフ協会公認競技

1990年8月3日(金) 4日(土) 5日(日) 白山カントリー倶楽部 主催／㈱学生援護会・北陸放送㈱

**Above: Posters for ladies' tournament and Japanese television.**

**Left: What do sumo wrestlers do after they retire to lose weight and stay fit? They play golf. Hiroshi Wajima, the great grand champion *(Yokozuna)* of the '70s is an example.**

**Opposite: Ayako Okamoto—popular Japanese export who draws large galleries wherever she plays. The state of New Jersey has a very large number of Japanese residents. Judging by the hordes she attracted at the Women's US Open in Edison, N.J. in 1990, most of them must have turned up.**

Shiba Driving Range
LeRoy Neiman 3 '91 Tokyo

## DRIVING RANGES

Driving ranges seem as prevalent in Tokyo as golf courses
are in Palm Springs or Scottsdale and are squeezed into every
available space all over the country.

   The golf craze has brought about indoor simulated-golf
establishments popping up all over New York and other Ameri-
can cities as well. Indoor golf, high tech inner-city country
clubs are with us thanks to the latest computer technology.

シティゴルフプラザ
City Golf Plaza
FUKUOKA Japan
LeRoy Neiman 3. '91

**Opposite:** The Shiba Golf, a three-tiered, curving driving range, situated in the shadow of the Tokyo Tower in central Tokyo. The facility is booked to capacity at all hours.

Driving golf balls out over parked cars in a parking lot is not unusual at this Fukuoka driving range. Any place a net can be strung up to catch balls is utilized. Lots of young Japanese couples date here.

## KAWANA

The numerous golf courses that ring
Mount Fuji during cherry-blossom time
bring to mind Hokusai's and Hiroshige's
woodblock print depictions of the peerless mountain and the life at its base.

Along the east coast of Izu—the
playground peninsula—positioned like
a citadel on a hilltop, sits the red-tile
roofed clubhouse of the Kawana Resorts
Golf Club overlooking the hilly Fuji
course facing Mount Fuji. The Fuji
course, with rolling steep hills and bunkers of volcanic black sand is one of the
most majestic and most difficult courses
in all of Japan.

One of Japan's old-line clubs, Kawana
dates back to the '20s and holds a
highly respected position among the
hard-driving corporate Nipponese.

# OLD ORCHARD

Japan's robust mountainous countryside provides magnificent terrain for transformation into prosperous snazzy golfing developments.

About an hour's drive northeast of traffic-snarled, jammed metropolitan Tokyo lies a spanking-new spectacular golf layout called "Old Orchard" with an imposing vanguard clubhouse only the Japanese could fathom. It's sort of a neo-Buddhist temple, or is it a new-fangled Imperial structure? Whatever—it is one glittering edifice built for the edification of golf, wealth, and well-being.

**PEBBLE BEACH GOLF LINKS**

The "Sistine Chapel of Golf." The most idyllic and most dramatic terrain of any course in the world, blending un-rivaled beauty with unbelievable weather. Pebble Beach sets the standard by which all other golf courses and holes are measured.

Amid a setting of extravagant vistas, cliffside fairways, sea-sloping greens, and spectacular sunsets, major tourna-ments are held here regularly.

Jack Nicklaus alone won the US Amateur, the US Open, and the Crosby three times here. Jack calls Pebble Beach "the best thinking-man's course in the country." In 1984, Jack told me "18 is the most spectacular par-5 hole on the face of the earth." The only problem? "Keeping it out of the blasted ocean."

From left—former president Gerald Ford, Nicklaus putting, Tom Watson in red, and Clint Eastwood.

View from
Room 112
the Lodge at Pebble Beach

## THE LODGE

Equally revered is the gracious and hospitable Lodge at Pebble Beach, offering an atmosphere of refinement and sophisticated, relaxed elegance. Since 1919 the Lodge has overlooked the Pebble Beach golf links, Carmel Bay, and the Santa Lucia Mountains. It lies within the Del Monte Forest on the rugged, craggy coast of California's Monterey peninsula.

The immediate view from the Terrace Lounge or the irresistible Club XIX sidewalk cafe is of the famous 18th. The green is floodlit after dark, bringing out the emerald-green and yellow of the waving pin flag and bringing back memories of great finishes to diners and guests in the window-walled salon.

### AT&T
### PEBBLE BEACH
### NATIONAL
### PRO-AM

JANUARY 29, 30, 31
FEBRUARY 1, 1987

PEBBLE BEACH
SPYGLASS HILL
CYPRESS POINT

### BING CROSBY
### NATIONAL
### PRO-AMATEUR
### GOLF CHAMPIONSHIP
FEBRUARY •2•3•4•5•1984
PEBBLE BEACH, CALIFORNIA

## $440,000 PRIZE MONEY
72 HOLES PLAYED ON PEBBLE BEACH
SPYGLASS HILL & CYPRESS POINT

FOR TICKET INFORMATION • CROSBY OFFICE, 479 PACIFIC
STREET • MONTEREY CA 93940 • (408) 649-1533 • TICKETS
AVAILABLE THROUGH BASS & TICKETRON SALES OUTLETS

16th at

Cypress

LeRoy Neiman

## CYPRESS

Along the serpentine 17-Mile Drive on the Monterey peninsula, heroic links overhang the Pacific's windswept shoreline. Lashed by waves, the rugged cliffs support the contorted cypress, twisted by the wind but clinging tenaciously to the soil—consistent with the hardy, adventurous golfers.

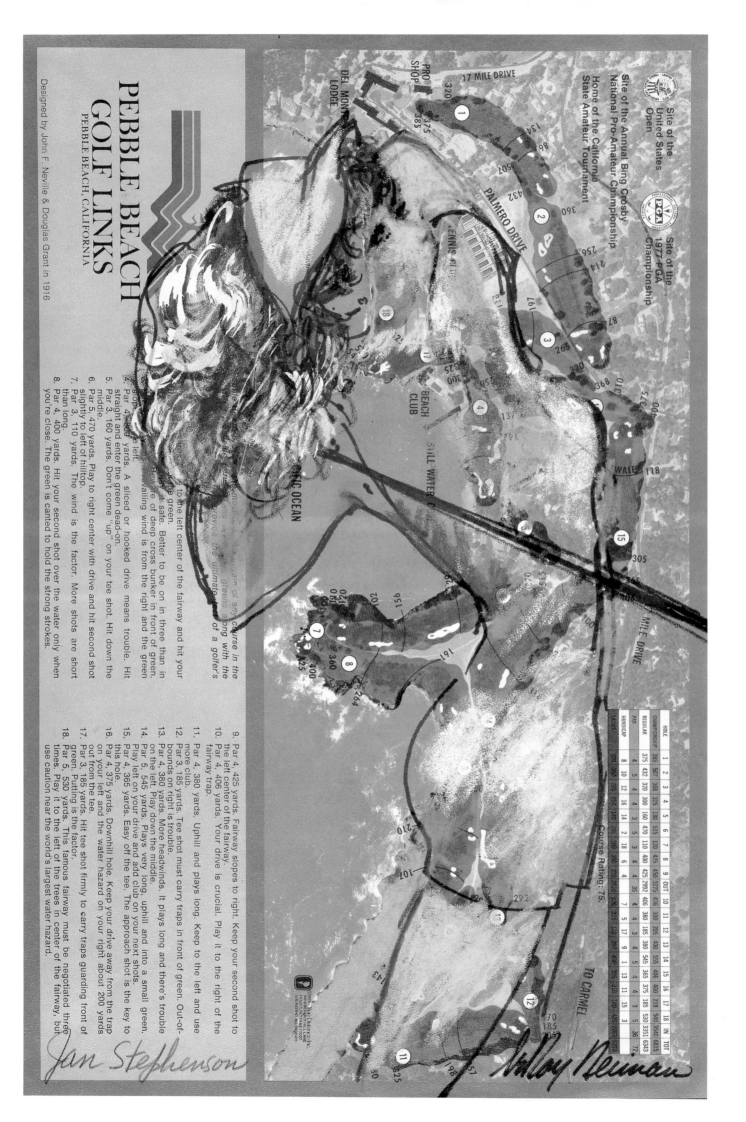

*Kathryn Crosby* *Bob Hope* Feb 2 1982
Monterey Peninsula

ED SCHOENFELD
Crosby Pro-Am
The Lodge at Pebble Beach *Ed Schoenfeld*
2-2-84

Lentil soupe du Jour

2-3-84

THE LODGE AT PEBBLE BEACH

## MONTEREY PENINSULA

## 16TH AT CYPRESS

Situated right there at what has been called the prettiest meeting of land and water in all of golf, veterans of the tour wars also call the 16th the most disastrous hole.

The 16th at Cypress is a par 3, 233 yards. To fail to drive across this churning inlet in the Pacific is a catastrophe. It's named the Bing Crosby Hole because Crosby made one of the few aces ever recorded here. Jerry Pate is seen in the painting making a hole-in-one, as he did in '78. In 1953 Porky Oliver scored a disastrous 16.

## SPYGLASS HILL

Rated the toughest course in California and in the top 100 in the world.

Spyglass Hill is named after the Spyglass Tavern, where, in Robert Louis Stevenson's *Treasure Island*, young Jim meets Long John Silver for the first time. The Spyglass was a little tavern with a large brass telescope for a sign. Its customers were raucous seafaring men.

The 1st hole, a par 5, with a 600-yard dogleg, is named "Treasure Island" after onetime resident Robert Louis Stevenson's classic novel. Hole 14—a par 5, at 555 yards the second longest on the course—is named "Long John Silver." Other holes are named for other characters and scenes in *Treasure Island*.

That's Tom Watson shooting—and could it be Robert Louis Stevenson making a cameo appearance on the left as Tom's caddy?

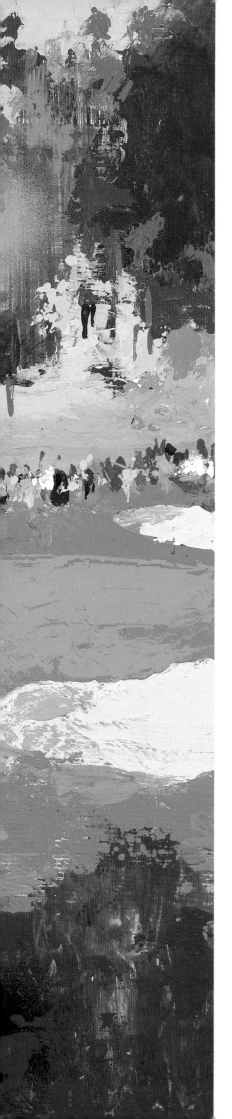

## THE MASTERS
## AUGUSTA NATIONAL

Where the sovereign order of golf's royalty reigns—the Versailles of golf. Its grandeur is the very essence of the ultimate in golf. Its cosmetic beauty, natural pictorial variety, regal conformation, and aesthetic appeal—its pomp and pageantry says it all.

It just wouldn't be The Masters without the drive up Magnolia Lane, the aging, churlish, curmudgeonly members, the elegant veranda, and the green blazers. You'll never find anything quite like the supreme big-time golf scene at The Masters

...where greenkeepers lie flat on their stomachs to clip the grass on the edges of the greens with scissors.

...where the water on the course is dyed blue.

...where club employees replace divots with green-colored soil.

With golf being a sort of religion to so many golfers, The Augusta National could well be called a sanctuary and the clubhouse its sacristy.

**The mighty leaderboard in the middle distance with the tall pines reflected in the water. From this distance, the gallery lined on both sides of the approach area and fringing the green is like a garden of flowers. The colorful attire of the spectators blends into the patches of azaleas that bloom around the course in the spring.**

Chairman Hord Hardin
Arnold Palmer.

Augusta National

## CLUBHOUSE AT AUGUSTA

In the area fronting the white wooden clubhouse that faces the glorious wide rolling course, the privileged patrons fraternize at tables and under umbrellas. Members sip juleps, fine wines, and great port from the club's cellars, observing the customs of etiquette and decorum as they are attended by courteous waiters. For the remainder of the tournament it becomes the commons of the principality of the royalistic Augusta National Golf Club.

Golf Club Club House

Bob Goalby

Augusta National Golf Club
April 9 1973

member Fred Brand Jr
Rules Committee for
Club Select Masters
Member

the oldest club in the world John Young member
Royal Burgess EDINBURGH scot

Above: The usual mood of high expectation at 9:30 one morning.

Left: In 1973, Bob Goalby —winner in '68; Fred Brand, Jr. —member, Rules Committee; John Young—visitor from the Royal Burgess in Edinburgh; Ben Crenshaw— winner-to-be in '84; Sam Snead (in yellow sweater)— winner three times ('49, '52, '54).

113

Above:
Pugnacious Monte
Carlo resident
Seve Balesteros
with over 50 wins,
"setting the table"
on the 1st tee.

Right: Master of
The Masters,
Nicklaus with
Jack, Jr., who
bears the Bear's
clubs.

Opposite: Nick
Faldo hitting for
what was to be his
2nd straight green
jacket conquest.

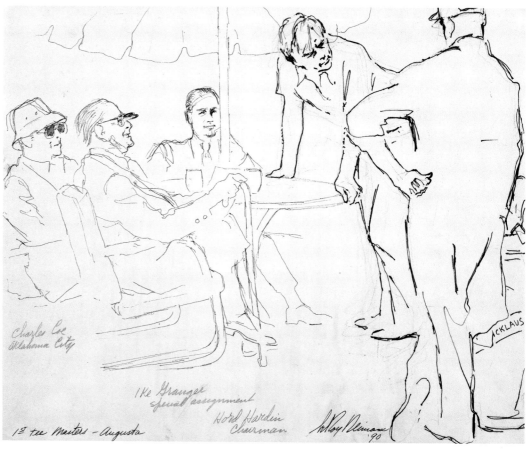

1ˢᵗ tee: Masters Augusta 1990     LeRoy Neiman     Nick Faldo

## TEEING GROUND

During the opening round, I settled
down at the 1st tee and watched each
pair sign in. I sketched most of the field
as each was announced, stepped up to
the tee, and played away.

**Opposite above:
Larry Mize—
1987 Masters
Champion, lives in
Utica, N.Y., but
was born in
Augusta 34 years
ago and so has a
feel for the region.**

Fans favor this location because of its proximity to the 1st and 10th tees and the 18th green. Chip shots are a tricky proposition even for high-velocity sand-blasters like Chip Beck of Georgia. The three-time college US Open champ, who shot a record-tying 59 in the 2nd round of the Las Vegas Invitational in 1991, chipping on, in two versions in the same situation, above and left.

During the 2nd
round I joined the
bleacher-ites at
this pivotal point
for about an hour
and a half, result-
ing in this water-
color. The ball can be
tracked coming in
and going away.

## LEADERBOARD

Corporate America's advertising has contributed to and benefited greatly from the popularity of golf. TV cameras pick up and follow the ball everywhere and cover just about all action and everyone on the course. The game's natural timing is perfect for commercial breaks.

The TV viewer and live spectator, as well as the golfers, have been spared distracting advertising pitches and images along the playing area. Racing cars are defaced with sponsor endorsements affixed all over their highly tuned machines. How about baseball, with product names plastered all over outfield fences and scoreboards? And then there's the logo desecration of the dignity of the prize ring. Few big-time sports are untouched.

Consider the horror if billboard-type advertising became an appendage to the golf leaderboards. With all apologies to The Masters officials, pray such an eventuality doesn't occur there or at any other of golf's untarnished environments.

As things are, scoreboards are removed at the completion of The Masters because members desire a pure, unadulterated, and unblemished landscape on which to play. It would seem that while they are playing they prefer not to be reminded of the numbers that have been put up on the boards during the tournament by the masters who play there.

# Pairings and Starting Time

## SATURDAY, APRIL 7, 1973

| A.M. | Caddie No. | | 1st Day | 2nd Day | Total | | Caddie No. | | 1st Day | 2nd Day | Total |
|------|-----------|-------------------|---------|---------|-------|---|-----------|------|---------|---------|-------|
| 10:08 | 77 | Bobby Nichols | | 72 | 154 | | | Jerry Heard | 76 | 75 | 151 |
| 10:16 | 81 | Al Geiberger | 75 | 76 | 151 | 34 | | | | | |
| 10:24 | 76 | Lou Graham | | | 150 | 79 | Bob Lunn | 76 | 74 | 150 |
| 10:32 | 71 | Sam Snead | | 76 | 150 | 4 | Miller Barber | 78 | 72 | 150 |
| 10:40 | 58 | Lee Trevino | 74 | 75 | 149 | 28 | Marvin M. Giles, III | 78 | 71 | 149 |
| 10:48 | 32 | Gene Littler | 77 | 72 | 149 | 33 | Lanny Wadkins | 75 | 74 | 149 |
| 10:56 | 52 | Arnold Palmer | | 72 | 149 | 48 | Bert Yancey | 75 | 74 | 149 |
| 11:04 | 40 | Ray Floyd | | 73 | 149 | 9 | John Schlee | 76 | 73 | 149 |
| 11:12 | 45 | Tom Weiskopf | 77 | 71 | 148 | 41 | Don Massengale | 74 | 74 | 148 |
| 11:20 | 72 | Art Wall, Jr. | 79 | 69 | 148 | 16 | Frank Beard | 73 | 75 | 148 |
| 11:28 | 46 | Roberto de Vicenzo (Argentina) | 74 | 74 | 148 | 59 | Paul Harney | 77 | 71 | 148 |
| 11:36 | 57 | Rod Funseth | 73 | 75 | 148 | 25 | Takaaki Kono (Japan) | 74 | 74 | 148 |
| 11:44 | 72 | Bruce Crampton (Australia) | 74 | 74 | 148 | 63 | Billy Casper | 75 | 73 | 148 |
| 11:52 | 12 | George Archer | 73 | 74 | 147 | 29 | Dave Hill | 77 | 70 | 147 |

| P.M. | | | | | | | | | | | |
|------|---|---|---|---|---|---|---|---|---|---|---|
| 12:00 | 14 | Cesar Sanudo | 72 | 75 | 147 | 74 | Charles Coody | 74 | 73 | 147 |
| 12:08 | 15 | Jim Colbert | 74 | 72 | 146 | 13 | Babe Hiskey | 74 | 73 | 147 |
| 12:16 | 54 | Hubert Green | 72 | 74 | 146 | 26 | Dave Stockton | 72 | 74 | 146 |
| 12:24 | 78 | Don January | 75 | 71 | 146 | 19 | David A. Graham (Australia) | 72 | 74 | 146 |
| 12:32 | 44 | Phil Rodgers | 71 | 75 | 146 | 27 | Lu Liang-Huan (Republic of China) | 74 | 72 | 146 |
| 12:40 | 1 | Jack Nicklaus | 69 | 77 | 146 | 20 | Steve Melnyk | | 74 | 146 |
| 12:48 | 18 | Bruce Devlin (Australia) | 73 | 72 | 145 | 36 | Ben Crenshaw | | 72 | 145 |
| 12:56 | 51 | Kermit Zarley | 74 | 71 | 145 | 5 | Martin R. West, III | 75 | 70 | 145 |
| 1:04 | 80 | Mason Rudolph | 72 | 72 | 144 | | Bob Charles (New Zealand) | 74 | 70 | 144 |
| 1:12 | 65 | Jim Jamieson | 73 | 71 | 144 | 30 | Gardner Dickinson | 74 | | 144 |
| 1:20 | 35 | Masashi Ozaki (Japan) | 69 | 74 | 143 | 64 | Johnny Miller | 75 | 69 | 144 |
| 1:28 | 21 | Peter Oosterhuis (England) | 73 | 70 | 143 | 62 | Grier Jones | 71 | 72 | 143 |
| 1:36 | 66 | Chi Chi Rodriguez | 72 | 70 | 142 | 69 | Bob Goalby | 73 | 70 | 143 |
| 1:44 | 60 | Bob Dickson | 70 | 71 | 141 | 70 | J. C. Snead | | 71 | 141 |
| 1:52 | 47 | Gay Brewer, Jr. | 75 | 66 | 141 | 68 | Tommy Aaron | | | 141 |

## INVITEES PRESENT WHO ARE NOT PARTICIPATING

Claude Harmon     Cary Middlecoff     Byron Nelson     Henry Picard

## HONORARY NON-COMPETING INVITEES WHO ARE PRESENT

| | | | |
|---|---|---|---|
| Jerry Barber | Vic Ghezzi | Fred McLeod | Denny Shute |
| Charles R. Coe | Bob Hamilton | Tony Manero | Jess W. Sweetser |
| Dow Finsterwald | M. R. "Chick" Harbert | Lloyd Mangrum | Lew Worsham, Jr. |
| John W. Fischer, Jr. | Jock Hutchison | Bob Rosburg | Charles R. Yates |
| Ed Furgol | | | |

Masters     Augusta National Golf Club     *LeRoy Neiman* '73

## OFF LIMITS

1973—I spent an early morning sketching Arnold Palmer in the impregnable Augusta clubhouse.

With Arnie's army waiting outside, I felt like an enlisted man in an officer's club, but I had credentials, being on assignment for *Golf Digest* magazine.

## ARNIE IN THE RAIN

Clubhouse porch at Augusta with Arnold Palmer, 10:15 A.M. On this dismal wet day, Arnie is scheduled to tee off at 10:58. From the white wooden porch of the modest Masters clubhouse, Arnie, with a brilliant azalea hanging overhead thriving in the rain, gloomily checks the incessant downpour as his legion of devoted followers, forming a congregation of believers, wait patiently for their hero so they may accompany him to the driving range.

Arnie concedes. Backed by his army, sheltered under their
umbrellas, Arnie is out in the open, driving in the rain.
Lee Trevino, in rainsuit, stands by, keeping him company.

I actually protected Arnie from and back to the clubhouse
under my umbrella—it also kept my sketch pad dry while
I sketched.

# PANORAMA FROM 10

Jack Nicklaus teeing off with Nick
Faldo, with Faldo's caddy, Fannie, and
Jack's son, Jack, Jr.

In the background, the practice
green spreads just behind Nicklaus, the
white clubhouse at his elbow. A player
and caddy are seen leaving the putting
area, headed for the 1st tee. To the left
of Faldo's head is the gallery around the
9th green, and in the middle distance
(in front of the cluster of oak trees) is
the 1st tee, with the fairway stretching
to the 1st hole at the far upper left.

Above: Greg
Norman whacking
the ball for my
benefit, I felt, just
for my sketch
(right).

Opposite: A bit
closer to the
Camellia Hole,
with Wayne Levi
in motion.

## THE 10TH FAIRWAY TO GREEN

Downhill all the way: At the top of his swing, Greg Norman
(opposite) takes his second shot downhill from the tee on the
10th fairway, 485 yards. Between the silk-like green and
breathtaking tall pines, rich-colored azalea beds blend with the
rainbow colors of the gallery.

Jack Nicklaus at Augusta
LeRoy Neiman

## PUTTING PRACTICE

Spectators line the ropes of the paddock to check out the players' form and attitude, just as racegoers check the thoroughbreds in the walking ring. Mostly they are just kibitzers or aficionados getting close enough to touch the pros.

The players socialize, check their green-reading skills, work on their stance, and polish their touch, their personalized technique, and the fundamentals of their strokes. Occasionally they break their concentration and stride to the ropes to shake hands and share words with friends or acquaintances.

If the power drive off the tee requires the same power as a home run swing in baseball, and if an iron target shot is as sharp as the hockey players' slapshot, then the putt requires the same concentration as the free throw in basketball.

*Fuzzy Zoeller*  *Jumbo Ozaki*    *Ben Crenshaw*    *craig Stadler*
*Hale Irwin*                      *Robert Gamez*    *Chris Patton*
*with glasses*                                       *South Carolina*

Left: "Close but no cigar."

Opposite: Every round and every tournament ends with a putt. Jack Nicklaus is a master at holing the ball.

Above: Hale Irwin —2-time US Open winner; Fuzzy Zoeller—from Indiana, US Open winner; Jumbo Ozaki—the pride of Japan; Ben Crenshaw—3-time NCAA champ, '84 Masters winner; Robert Gamez— from Las Vegas, who obviously prefers golf greens to gambling-table green; Craig Stadler—'82 Masters winner; Chris Patton—'91 amateur champion.

## OAKMONT

Oakmont Country Club outside Pittsburgh is nearly 90 years old and has the reputation of being possibly the most difficult course in the world. It boasts terrorizing, enormous, high, tilting greens and deep or huge or furrowed bunkers of which there are about 200, including the famous Church Pews and Big Mouth.

The oil I did at Oakmont at the 1983 US Open depicts Watson teeing off, flanked by Balesteros and Calvin Peete. I stationed myself well below but within a few yards of the 10th tee platform. The tee shot balls whistled by just overhead as I made my studies and sketches. The view in the painting takes in the stately period clubhouse on the left with 1st Oakmont US Open winner Tommy Armour on the huge back-portion putting practice green, with the 9th hole just in front. Directly behind Calvin Peete to the left is an imposing group. Teeing off is Palmer with Nicklaus and Snead.

To the far right on the 18th green, other US Open champs from the past— Ben Hogan, 1953 US Open winner, here hitting out of the bunker; Bobby Jones in knickers; and Larry Nelson.

A dealer demanded I remove Peete from prominence in the painting, claiming the presence of a black player would damage sales. I refused. The original was scooped up, and the 350-print silkscreen edition, based on the oil, sold out immediately.

18th Hole
Oakmont Country Club    Larry Nelson
1983 U.S. Open
Pittsburg

# OAKMONT

Ray Floyd '83

Opposite: The man who was to win the '83 US Open, Larry Nelson, pitching out of a deep trap bunker on 18.

Seve Ballesteros
the favorite

Tommy Nakajima
Japanese – First US Open

US Open Oakmont 1983

133

# FLORIDA GOLF

## THE BOCA RATON GOLF CLUB

### "THE ELEGANT PLACE TO PLAY"

In this playground oasis of the rich, Florida snowbirds patiently line up at the 1st tee in their pink, non-cranky electric "club carts" with their bingo-like score cards clipped to the steering wheel.

That's "Slamming Sammy" Snead, who was the director of golf operations and teacher at the Boca Raton Course from the mid-'50s through the '60s, being snapped by a "just happy to be here" waiting couple.

The golfers don't mind waiting to tee off. It's like being in a traffic backup along the nearby Intracoastal Waterway, waiting for the Boca drawbridge to lower over the river—it goes with the territory.

Participation can be sedentary here—all part of the game. Pink golf carts or no, Arnold Palmer said, a few years back, "If you need a golf cart...don't golf."

Sam Snead

THE CLOISTER · THE TOWER · THE GOLF VILLAS · THE BOCA BEACH CLUB

'91

Andy Bean
Imperial Lakes Country Club
Lakeland, Florida

LeRoy Neiman '83

## FLORIDIANS

Miami resident Ray Floyd, a Masters, US Open, PGA, you-name-it champ. His off-the-tee drives are home runs. His woods are doubles off the fences. His iron shots are sharp singles through the infield. His lob shots are Texas League hits. His putt has the finesse of a bunt.

Georgia-born Florida resident Andy Bean, 1975 US Amateur champ. A kiloton driver of explosive force. As is the form, Andy selects his driver from the bag, and then removes the cover jacket.

## SEMINOLE COUNTRY CLUB
## NORTH PALM BEACH

Big-time private course. Open November to May with no big-time tournaments.

Winged Foot caddies go south to ply their trade in the winter, while egrets strut right on the course to show off their long, provocative, graceful plumes during mating season.

The 14th hole stopped me in my tracks because of this odd tree combination—a palm growing right out of the trunk of another tree.

Four greens are visible from this position, with the 11th flag seen directly behind in the painting surrounded by palms and seminole pines. The great hole is 6—par 4, 388 yards with 11 bunkers.

The Seminole Indians formed by splitting away from the Creek. Seminole means "Seceders." The Muskogean people of Florida are a Seminole people. Muskogees is the language of some Seminoles. However, the lingo in the clubhouse is strictly golfese with maybe a bit of profanity out on the course.

LeRoy Neiman '91    Seminole, Florida

## THE SEMINOLE TRIBESMAN

Rather than lofting the ball high over the tree with a grass-clipping cut at the bottom of his swing, the player gouges a deep divot, hitting a low, running shot under the hanging branches toward the well-trapped green.

Seminole

Falling short of the 14th green, the ball drops in the leading
edge of the bunker. As the member is in the process of spoon-
ing his ball with an eye on the flag, his caddy's distracted eye
follows an egret tracking in the sand.

Azinger                    LeRoy Neiman '91

Corey Pavin and caddies

Fred Couples Palm Beach on the fairway in the rain

GOLF SHOWER

**Above: Golf shower, Palm Beach. Fred "Boom-Boom" Couples swinging in the rain, with Corey Pavin looking on.**

**Opposite: Blue-chip player, sandman Paul "A Zinger" Azinger— he's a pride of Florida, from A to Z.**

145

LeRoy Neiman '91

# WINGED FOOT—BALTUSROL

New York State has Shinnecock Hills in Southampton, and New Jersey has the Pine Valley Golf Club in Clementon. But there are also two picturesque courses a commute away from New York City, Winged Foot and Baltusrol.

Winged Foot is in Mamaroneck, New York. The upper and lower courses were built in 1923 and were created by architect Arthur Tillinghast, who also created Baltusrol, its sister course in Springfield, New Jersey. Baltusrol's east and west courses were built in 1920.

Winged Foot's 9th hole is par 4, 456 yards—one of the toughest tests anywhere.

The golf clubhouse, set in the midst of magnificent greens, is modeled after the great English manor houses. In fact, golf club architecture in general is similar to domestic architecture on a grand scale—golf clubs are like oversize mansions on oversize lawns.

In the painting, after two wood shots a member goes for a birdie on the undulating narrow green. Though hopeful, he'll settle happily for par. The prestigious clubhouse serves as the backdrop.

## WINGED FOOT

A few steps from Winged Foot's English-style clubhouse is the 10th tee, 190 yards, par 3. Every aspect of the hole is beautifully proportioned.

Equally eye-arresting is the enormous famed elm right next to the clubhouse, overhanging the 10th east green, casting a shadow in the A.M. The majestic elm is the patriarch of Winged Foot's friendly trees. As with so many trees that line the fairway, its branches spread, and foliage plays a key part in the player's strategy.

Talk about class—not a lock is to be seen in the men's locker room.

One member tells how, in 1991 on the 5th tee, he took his cellular phone out of his hip pocket, and made a call to stay abreast of a company merger. Upon completion of his conversation, his caddy approached: "Sir, can I use your phone? I gotta call my probation officer."

Mighty clubs like Winged Foot offer misdirected youth a second chance and the opportunity to relate to and be in direct contact with successful, responsible men and women in a discretionary environment.

Winged Foot Golf Club
Mamaroneck N.Y.
LeRoy Neiman '91

Baltusrol Golf Club

LeRoy Neiman '91

## BALTUSROL

Baltusrol Golf Club has an abundance of blue-blood members, "dream holes," and trees that are full and varied along the graceful fairways. River birch, linden, and ginkgo trees abound, plus there's an extraordinary Douglas fir that stands guard next to the Tudor clubhouse. A luscious spread of lawn swoops down from the clubhouse patio with a panorama that includes the famous 4th, which is entirely across water, with a rock escarpment before the green. Tom Watson made a hole-in-one on this 194-yarder. From the upper clubhouse terrace, you can clearly see the towers of Manhattan looming.

After a morning's play, lunch on the patio—an avocado, French Brie, and watercress sandwich with a "transfusion" (made of grape juice and ginger ale) or a "Morrison" (a lemon, orange, and cranberry drink) hits the spot with a side order of either onion rings or sautéed onions from the same rich soil of the area.

Golf carts are discouraged, and the use of caddies, encouraged. For the members' convenience the scorecard bears two slits for the insertion of the marking pencil so that it won't fall and get lost during the round.

**That's Arnie—who else?—classically driving off the 1st tee, with a casual Fred Couples on deck and the magnificent clubhouse as a backdrop.**

Below: LeRoy with caddy at Shek O, Hong Kong.

Right: At the 1st green with tree easel at Spyglass.

Left above: Sketching Nicklaus on 17 at Pebble.

Left: With film crew at Old Orchard, outside Tokyo.

Above: Walking the course at Kawana Fuji course, Japan.

Left: On 1st tee at
US Open,
Oakmont.

Below: With
bravura waiter
Harold and
William S. Morris III
at The Masters,
Augusta.

Left: Working at
Old Orchard,
outside Tokyo.

A reward kiss
from Kathy Crosby
on the terrace at
Pebble.

Right: On location
in the rain at
Kawana Fuji
course, Japan.

153

## RISK TAKERS

One afternoon in the summer of 1990, record honcho Martin Bandier phoned my studio requesting a painting of his partner playing golf—the partner being Charles Koppelman, chairman of New York–based SBK Records, a music-publishing, record-producing, and talent-management big-time hot-label company.

The money was persuasive, and the commission was accepted. It was to be his 50th birthday present. I had never seen or met Koppelman so photos were taken for my use; they proved he had good form and class. It was swing time.

**Above left:**
**Martin Bandier.**

**Above right:**
**Charles Koppelman.**

A month later, I personally delivered the painting, and both hard-hitting marketing impresario partners were beside themselves.

Then—listen to this—nearly a year later, Koppelman phoned. Would I do the same of partner Bandier? Same deal—now it's *his* birthday present. The photos showed he was a power hitter. The result was positive. The whole experience was a hoot and rewarding for all.

**Right: Included for balance, a 1980s conté crayon drawing of a single-digit handicap player, celebrity real-estate developer Donald Trump in his 30s. Ask Donald—isn't it a maxim of golf that the course is a great place to do business?**

Donald Trump

LeRoy Neiman

'86

THE
VANISHING
BREED

# CADDIES

In the tour wars, a golfer's personal resources are his clubs. The foot soldier bearer-of-arms who carries the munitions of battle totes 14 clubs on a round, or up to the *22* allowed for practice. Whew!

The caddy, a vanishing breed, is hired not only to carry a player's clubs and to find the ball, but because he knows the distance to the hole and considers it his duty to keep the player up and settle him down when he is hot.

The caddy will hold the flag while holding the pin. He will not stand too close to the hole when taking out or replacing the flagstick, and then he properly replaces it before the players leave the green.

A companion, assistant, and confidant, the time-honored caddy has no parallel in any other sport, unless one harks back to the relationship of the old life-threatening two-seater racing machines of driver and mechanic at Indy in the '30s or today's road-race rally's driver and navigator teams. The word "caddy" comes from the French *cadet*, meaning "little chief." A far cry from the batboy of baseball.

Many of the game's top players started as kids hiring out as caddies in exalted private country clubs. Later, they used the facilities, and went on to become top tour professionals. Thanks then to their renown they made full circle back to these very clubs, this time being hired as resident pros and teachers, members ex officio.

158

# Pairings and Starting Time

## THURSDAY, APRIL 5, 1990

| A.M. | Caddie No. | | | Caddie No. | |
|------|------|------|------|------|------|
| 8:30 | 94 | Gene Sarazen | 95 | | Sam Snead |
| 8:45 | 57 | Tom Byrum | 14 | | Andy Bean |
| 8:53 | 69 | George Archer | 10 | | Timothy L. Halby |
| 9:01 | 39 | Tommy Aaron | 35 | | Doug Ford |
| 9:09 | 38 | Hubert Green | 11 | | John Huston |
| 9:17 | 67 | Billy Casper | 19 | | Daniel W. Green |
| 9:25 | 22 | Don Pooley | 56 | | Curt Byrum |
| 9:33 | 66 | Ray Floyd | 75 | | David Frost (South Africa) |
| 9:41 | | Tom Purtzer | 49 | | Brian Claar |
| 9:49 | 63 | Tom Jacson | 28 | | Ian Baker-Finch (Australia) |
| 9:57 | | Andy North | 21 | | Bob Tway |
| 10:05 | | Larry Nelson | 52 | | John Mahaffey |
| 10:13 | | Scott Hoch | 55 | | Ronan Rafferty (N. Ireland) |
| 10:21 | 68 | Tim Simpson | 9 | | Ted Schulz |
| 10:29 | 20 | Jeff Sluman | 34 | | Tommy Armour, III |
| 10:37 | 51 | Steve Jones | 45 | | Ken Green |
| 10:45 | 8 | Arnold Palmer | 27 | | James W. Taylor |
| 10:53 | 53 | Peter Jacobsen | 74 | | Mark McCumber |
| 11:01 | 30 | Sandy Lyle (Scotland) | 15 | | Jodie Mudd |
| 11:09 | 25 | Mark O'Meara | 17 | | Blaine McCallister |
| 11:17 | 58 | Fuzzy Zoeller | 8 | | Peter Senior (Australia) |
| 11:25 | 76 | Gay Brewer, Jr. | 33 | | Craig Parry (Australia) |
| 11:33 | 41 | Curtis Strange | 5 | | Stephen C. Dodd (Wales) |
| 11:41 | | OPEN | | | |
| 11:49 | 36 | Lanny Wadkins | 13 | | Chip Beck |
| 11:57 | 60 | Larry Mize | 12 | | Wayne Grady (Australia) |
| **P.M.** | | | | | |
| 12:05 | 7 | Bernhard Langer (West Germany) | 64 | | Tom Kite |
| 12:13 | 24 | Mike Donald | 6 | | Dan Forsman |
| 12:21 | 79 | Lee Trevino | 72 | | Wayne Levi |
| 12:29 | 78 | Payne Stewart | 26 | | Ian Woosnam (Wales) |
| 12:37 | 77 | Hal Sutton | 4 | | Robert Gamez |
| 12:45 | 50 | Bill Glasson | 31 | | Leonard Thompson |
| 12:53 | 54 | Craig Stadler | 3 | | Naomichi Ozaki (Japan) |
| 1:01 | | Nick Faldo (England) | 47 | | Christopher L. Patton |
| 1:09 | | Ben Crenshaw | 29 | | Jose-Maria Olazabal (Spain) |
| 1:17 | 17 | Mark Lye | 40 | | David Rummells |
| 1:25 | 82 | Jack Nicklaus | 83 | | Greg Norman (Australia) |
| 1:33 | | OPEN | | | |
| 1:41 | 84 | Mark Calcavecchia | | | Paul Azinger |
| 1:49 | 65 | Gary Player (South Africa) | 16 | | David Ishii |
| 1:57 | 61 | Charles Coody | | | Masashi Ozaki (Japan) |
| 2:05 | 32 | Severiano Ballesteros (Spain) | 62 | | Fred Couples |
| 2:13 | 44 | Donnie Hammond | | | Scott Simpson |
| 2:21 | 18 | Mike Hulbert | 59 | | Mike Reid |
| 2:29 | 42 | Tom Pernice, Jr. | 23 | | Bill Britton |
| | 85 | Tony Sills | | | |

## INVITEES PRESENT WHO ARE NOT PARTICIPATING

| | | |
|---|---|---|
| Bob Goalby | Byron Nelson | |
| Herman Keiser | Henry Picard | Sam Snead |

## HONORARY NON-COMPETING INVITEES WHO ARE PRESENT

| | | |
|---|---|---|
| Stewart M. Alexander | Marvin M. Giles III | Fred Ridley |
| Charles R. Coe | David Graham | Ken Venturi |
| Gary Cowan | Jay Hebert | Tom Weiskopf |
| Dow Finsterwald | Tony Jacklin | Lew Worsham, Jr. |
| Ed Furgol | Jerry Pate | Charles R. Yates |

Fanny Sunesson

NICK Faldo
Masters – Augusta

LeRoy Neiman '90

LeRoy Neiman    June '85    6th green    Gávea Golf Course
Rio

LeRoy Neiman
79

Jack
Nicklaus

caddy
Angelo

tee in mouth
Pencil back of ear
cigar in hand

LeRoy Neiman '79

Lee Trevino

caddy
Neil

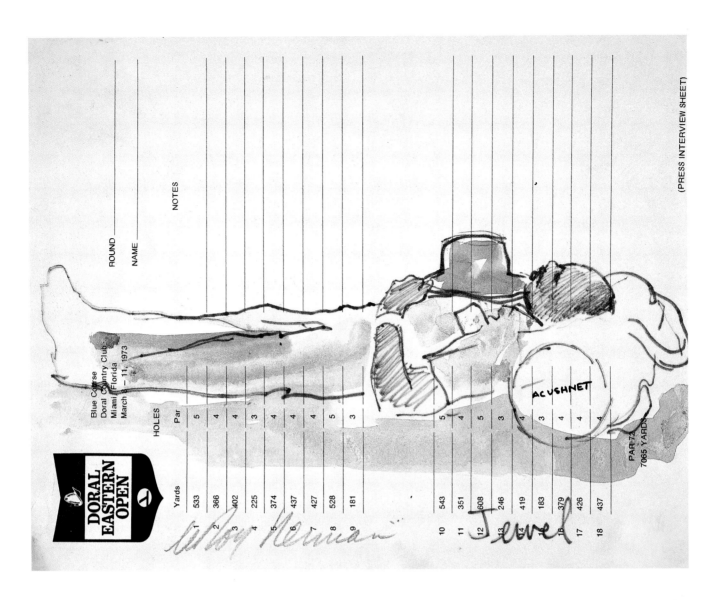

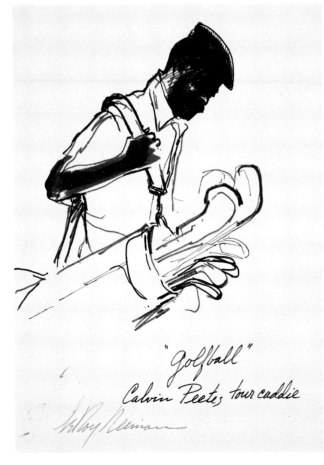

"Golfball"
Calvin Peete's tour caddie

# JACK

Nicklaus and Arnold Palmer are feeling well and playing well. Never before or since Hogan and Snead dominated the early '50s have any two players equaled or even come close to the excitement Jack and Arnie have caused.

In the tradition of incomparable duos such as DiMaggio-Williams, Ali-Frazier, Chamberlain-Russell, we have Palmer-Nicklaus as towering cynosures in all big-time sports. They remain the center of attraction wherever they clobber the ball—the most observed of all.

A fierce, decisive, tough competitor, Jack has had a distinctive, consistent image since before he won his 1st Masters in '63 at age 23. (He scored 51 for 9 holes at age 10.) From crewcut through the moderately long, windblown, dry-haired Kennedy look, the "Golden Bear" carried away every trophy and title there seems to be, from college to amateur to pro.

The Nicklaus stupendous drive is a picture to behold. I've sketched it live in profile, from behind, and on the oblique from the front, trying in a quick sketch to measure up to the authority and power of his release. A guardhouse gate attendant at Augusta told me he has seen many a Nicklaus ball struck from the driving range sail out over his head into the traffic on Washington Road.

# ARNIE

, the deity of golf in the '60s—actually the age of Palmer—started with his 1st Masters win in '58. Arnie's army is legend, his ladies' auxiliary gallery and his countless die-hard idolaters, the likes of which may never be seen again. He personalized tournament golf; he made it more than golf by adding his accommodating, gracious, honest, outgoing personality to some very daring, spectacular golf.

Arnie, a former caddy from Latrobe, Penn., son of a greenkeeper and teaching pro, broke 100 for 18 holes at age 7. He remains loyal to his beginnings. After having conquered and designed courses all over the world, Arnie still calls Latrobe his home base.

I've sketched him during the heat of concentration, maintaining his remarkable rapport with his legion of fans, and I've sketched his legendary hitching-up-the-trousers routine.

I've painted his form—from the expressionistic lunging swing to the familiar putting stance, powerful shoulders bunched. Then the finale, the Palmer putt holed and his troops marching in total disorder, tagging along as their commandant leaves the green.

Always the regular guy.

Two regular guys—Jack and Arnie.

Red Smith

Press Room

Jack interviewed after 65 round.

Nicklaus

Nicklaus    Westchester

1:45 P.M.

# MEDIA MIGHTS

Darlings of the 4th estate, Jack and Arnie magnetize the
press corps and combat-field photographers.

**Nicklaus in the
interview tent
after winning
at Westchester
in 1972.**

**Palmer takes a
breather at
Shinnecock, 1986.**

# THE OLD GUARD

Golf threesome—
Jack going for the
flag. A classic
Palmer stance
on the right, with
Lee Trevino adding
his presence on
the left.

## THE NEW BREED

With golf burgeoning all over the world, and so many thousands seriously taking up the game, left-handed hitters and long-ball hitters are on the increase on the tour and in golf dufferdom.

Be prepared to see a lot more lefties and power hitters emulating the spectacular Phil Mickleson and John Daly, both in their 20s. Mickleson, a 6′ 2″ clean-cut southpaw from San Diego, distinguished himself in NCAA and amateur tournaments. The long-driving Bunyanesque folk-hero powerhouse, Daly was the sensational 1991 PGA winner in his rookie year.

They are today's typical pacesetters, members of the new breed who hold to their natural talents and play to their strengths.

# Golf's "Fore-Letter" Words

| | |
|---|---|
| **ACHE** | feeling one gets from three-putting |
| **AWAY** | person whose ball lies most distant from hole |
| **BACK** | usually holes 10–18 |
| **BALL** | ammo used in golf war |
| **BANK** | where balls are deposited when not on green |
| **BARK** | what comes off tree after being hit by club |
| **BIRD** | a rare species of a score—one under par |
| **CARD** | the filing process used to record scores |
| **CART** | gas or electric vehicle used to speed up play |
| **CHIP** | a short shot often ending up in the hole |
| **CLUB** | one of 14 instruments selected for a shot |
| **DEEP** | location of ball in high grass |
| **DOWN** | position of head on every shot |
| **DRAW** | manmade curve on a long hit |
| **DROP** | the only thing that's free in golf |
| **DUNE** | an ocean-made sand mound found on links courses |
| **FACE** | the front part of the hitting instrument |
| **FADE** | another motion of the ball to get around an obstacle |
| **FEES** | cost of a round |
| **FEET** | used in lieu of golf carts |
| **FIRM** | condition of green during droughts |
| **FIVE** | the most par strokes on a given hole |
| **FLAG** | indicator of hole location on green |

| | |
|---|---|
| **FORE** | early-warning system used by golfers |
| **FORM** | exhibited by pros during tournament |
| **FOUR** | the number of strokes allowed on the majority of holes |
| **GAME** | an agreement among members to play together |
| **GOLF** | an ancient game of skill carried across the ocean |
| **GOSH** | word seldom heard on course |
| **GRIP** | method of holding onto club |
| **HDCP** | what the average golfer considers his distance from being a pro |
| **HEAD** | bottom portion of every golf utensil |
| **HEEL** | end of club that, when hit, gives poor direction |
| **HERO** | the golf widow (or widower) |
| **HIGH** | what one experiences after making a birdie |
| **HILL** | the most tiring aspect of golf when walking |
| **HITS** | the act of striking the ball |
| **HOLE** | the circular receptacle for the ball |
| **HOOK** | an inadvertent flight of the ball to the left |
| **IRON** | instrument used for shorter, more accurate shots |
| **LAKE** | receptacle for balls on way to hole |
| **LAND** | what you stand on when looking for balls in lake |
| **LAWN** | manicured grass around clubhouse entrance |
| **LEAF** | rule in golf that comes into play in the fall |
| **LIES** | manner in which ball addresses ground |
| **LINE** | shortest distance from ball to hole |

|  |  |
|------|------------|
| **LOBS** | shots usually found where ball travels on a high arc |
| **LOCH** | wet Scottish area where winds develop |
| **LOFT** | slant of club face that dictates how high the ball will travel |
| **LONG** | the distance beyond the hole a ball travels |
| **MARK** | the indication left on the green when ball is removed |
| **MOOR** | birthplace of golf |
| **NECK** | the portion of the hitting instrument found between club head and shaft |
| **NINE** | the number of holes in one half of a golf round |
| **OPEN** | the pro showcase |
| **PAIR** | what partners in golf are called |
| **PATH** | a well-worn route between holes |
| **PINE** | type of tree that lines most fairways |
| **PLAY** | the verb referring to the noun golf |
| **PLAY** | what transpires after teeing up 1st ball |
| **POND** | a body of water usually found between ball and hole |
| **PROS** | those whose office is on the golf course |
| **PULL** | a poorly hit ball, usually out of bounds |
| **PUSH** | another type of poorly hit ball |
| **PUTT** | the gentlest of all golf strokes |
| **RAIN** | the secret ingredient of perfect fairways |
| **ROAD** | a wide, usually asphalt or concrete, path leading to a golf club |
| **ROCK** | an object usually found in poor golfing terrain |
| **ROLL** | action of ball as it progresses toward hole |
| **RULE** | the law of the fairways |
| **SAND** | a colorless, odorless, desolate feature found around greens |
| **SHAG** | an ancient caddy ritual of returning a ball hit in a practice session |
| **SHOE** | when worn with another, allows golfer to play properly |
| **SHOT** | the result of a swing |
| **SLAM** | the grandest of all accomplishments |
| **SOAR** | direction of ball hit by a high iron |
| **SOCK** | piece of clothing that protects foot from shoe |
| **SOCK** | a manner of hitting the ball |
| **SODA** | refreshment sought after 9 holes |
| **SOIL** | chunk of divot |
| **SOLE** | bottom of club |
| **SORE** | condition of hands if wrong grip is used |
| **SPIN** | action put on ball by pro |
| **SUNK** | disappearance of ball on green |
| **TEES** | area where play begins on each hole |
| **TENT** | temporary housing found on fairways during tournaments |
| **TOUR** | route pros take during summer months |
| **TRAP** | area that holds sand |
| **TREE** | tallest growth found along fairways |
| **TURF** | an agronomist's noun for grass |
| **USGA** | ruling body of rules makers |
| **VIEW** | sight from tees |
| **WALK** | as opposed to ride in cart |
| **WEED** | unimproved grass |
| **WHIF** | unmoved ball after a swing |
| **WIND** | force of air affecting ball's flight |
| **WOOD** | instrument that can move the ball further than an iron |
| **YARD** | standard measurement in US golf |
| **YIPS** | when hand and eye movements fight each other |
| **ZERO** | a pro's handicap |

Note: Not included—the many self-deprecating four-letter words uttered under breath in golf.

# THE
# RETRIEVER

**A hungry dog
hunts best.**

## PHOTO CREDITS

All photographs taken by Anthony Holmes except those listed below:

Mike Conroy: 52 top, 52–53, 53 top, 53 center, 152 center, 153 below left (2)

Jim Mahoney: 152 above left

Lynn Quayle: 7 (2), 8 (2), 9 (2), 40, 52 center, 52 below, 53 below, 74, 126, 151, 152 above right, 152 below left, 153 above right, 153 center, 153 below right

Paul A. Selvaggio: 153 above left

Ken Zeran: 65, 68

## ACKNOWLEDGMENTS

I'd like to thank my kind friends Lynn Quayle and Charles H. McCabe, Jr.